Ant Middleton

Anthony Middleton, born on September 22, 1980, in Portsmouth, Hampshire, grew up in France, where he developed a profound sense of adventure and resilience. These qualities would later define his career as a soldier, adventurer, and television personality.

At 17, Middleton joined the British Army in 1998, beginning his military journey with the 9 Parachute Squadron Royal Engineers. His early service saw him deployed on tours of duty in Northern Ireland in 1999 and Macedonia in 2001. Seeking new challenges, he left the army in 2002, only to return to military life by enlisting in the Royal Marines on May 2, 2005. His dedication and prowess were evident as he passed the grueling 32-week commando course on January 20, 2006, earning the prestigious King's Badge for best all-around recruit.

Middleton's first tour in Afghanistan in 2007 with D Company, 40 Commando, further solidified his reputation as a formidable soldier. In 2008, he joined the Special Boat Service (SBS), the elite unit of the UK Special Forces, where he served with distinction for four years. After leaving the military, Middleton transitioned to the private sector, working as a security guard for VIPs and a security expert in South Africa and West Africa.

In 2015, Middleton's life took a turn towards the limelight when he became the Chief Instructor on the Channel 4 television series SAS: Who Dares Wins. The show, which simulated the intense selection process of the Special Forces, quickly became a hit and catapulted Middleton into the public eye. His role on the show lasted until 2021, during which he became known for his no-nonsense attitude and leadership skills.

Middleton's television career expanded with his role as the Captain in the adventure/reality-show Mutiny, aired in February 2017. The show was a re-enactment of the historic Mutiny on the Bounty, and Middleton described the experience as "mentally speaking, the hardest thing I've ever done." He also starred in the survival show Escape and climbed Mount Everest for the TV show Extreme Everest with Ant Middleton in 2018, nearly losing his life in a blizzard during the descent.
Despite his television success, Middleton faced controversies. In March 2021, Channel 4 dropped him over personal conduct issues. Nevertheless, he maintained his position as the host of SAS Australia: Who Dares Wins on the Seven Network and began hosting the reality adventure show Million Dollar Island, also for Seven.
Middleton's literary career is equally impressive. In 2017, he co-authored SAS: Who Dares Wins: Leadership Secrets from the Special Forces. His autobiography, First Man In: Leading from the Front, published in 2018, became a Number 1 Sunday Times best-seller. His subsequent books, The Fear Bubble (2019) and Zero Negativity (2020), also topped the Sunday Times best-seller chart. Middleton features in Coach Mike Chadwick's audiobook The Red On Revolution, published in 2022.

In May 2018, Middleton summited Mount Everest with Ed Wardle, a feat that took five and a half weeks and almost cost them their lives due to a severe blizzard. In November 2019, Middleton was appointed Chief Cadet and Honorary Captain in the Royal Navy's Volunteer Cadet Corps, a position he left nine months later amid controversy over a Twitter comment regarding Black Lives Matter protesters and the English Defence League.
Middleton's personal life has seen its share of turbulence. In 2013, he was convicted of unlawful wounding and common assault of police officers during a nightclub incident, for which he served four months of a 14-month sentence. Despite these challenges, Middleton has remained a prominent public figure, known for his resilience and determination.

As of 2023, Middleton announced his role in the film Shelter, directed by Scott Vickers. His filmography includes several television series such as SAS: Who Dares Wins, Mutiny, Escape, and Extreme Everest with Ant Middleton, as well as hosting roles on Celebrity SAS: Who Dares Wins and Ant Middleton and Liam Payne: Straight Talking. He continues to host SAS Australia and Million Dollar Island.

Middleton's journey from a soldier to a celebrated adventurer and television personality is a testament to his indomitable spirit and relentless pursuit of excellence. His story inspires many, showcasing the power of resilience, leadership, and the will to overcome life's greatest challenges.

Middleton's story of transformation and achievement extends beyond his military and television careers. His experiences have translated into motivational speaking engagements and live tours, where he shares his insights on leadership, resilience, and mental fortitude. His tours, including "An Evening with Ant Middleton" in 2018, "Mind Over Muscle" in 2019, and "Zero Negativity" in 2021, have captivated audiences across the UK and beyond.

In addition to his live tours, Middleton has authored several books that delve into the mindset and principles that have guided his life. His non-fiction works include "Mental Fitness: 15 Rules to Strengthen Your Body and Mind" (2021) and "Mission: Total Resilience" (2022), both of which provide practical advice on developing mental toughness and resilience. He has also ventured into fiction, with novels like "Cold Justice" (2021) and "Red Mist" (2023), showcasing his storytelling abilities.

Middleton's dedication to inspiring others is evident in his collaborations and media appearances. He has been featured in various documentaries and interviews, discussing his life experiences and the lessons he has learned along the way. His commitment to positive thinking and overcoming adversity resonates with many, making him a sought-after speaker and mentor.

Despite facing personal and professional challenges, Middleton's resilience has remained unwavering. His ability to bounce back from setbacks and continue striving for success is a testament to his inner strength. This resilience was particularly evident during his time on "Mutiny," where he and his crew faced extreme physical and mental challenges, yet persevered through sheer determination.

Middleton's role as an Honorary Captain in the Royal Navy's Volunteer Cadet Corps, though short-lived, highlights his ongoing commitment to supporting and mentoring young people. His involvement in various charitable initiatives and community projects further demonstrates his dedication to giving back and making a positive impact on society.

In his personal life, Middleton's family remains a cornerstone of his support system. While details of his family life are kept relatively private, his public persona reflects a deep appreciation for the values of loyalty, courage, and perseverance instilled in him from a young age.

As Middleton continues to navigate new ventures and opportunities, his story serves as an inspiration to many. From the battlefields of Afghanistan to the peaks of Mount Everest, and from reality television to bestselling books, Anthony Middleton's journey is a powerful reminder of the human capacity for resilience, growth, and transformation. His legacy is one of courage, leadership, and an unwavering belief in the potential within each of us to overcome obstacles and achieve greatness.

Middleton's journey did not stop at television, books, and live tours. He has also become a significant figure in the realm of adventure and survival training. His hands-on approach and experience have led him to create training programs and workshops designed to instill resilience, leadership, and survival skills in participants. These programs have been well-received, attracting a diverse audience ranging from corporate teams to individuals seeking personal development.

One of Middleton's notable contributions to this field is the establishment of the "Ant Middleton Adventure Academy." This academy offers immersive experiences that challenge participants physically and mentally, mirroring the intense environments Middleton has faced throughout his career. Through these adventures, he teaches the importance of teamwork, mental fortitude, and the ability to thrive under pressure.

Middleton's influence extends to the digital realm, where he engages with a broad audience through social media. His motivational posts, videos, and live sessions provide daily doses of inspiration and practical advice to his followers. He uses these platforms to share insights, answer questions, and connect with fans worldwide, fostering a community of individuals striving for self-improvement and resilience.

In recent years, Middleton has also embraced the role of a mentor and coach for upcoming adventurers and aspiring television personalities. He leverages his extensive experience to guide and support those entering the competitive world of adventure television. His mentorship has helped shape the careers of several rising stars, further cementing his legacy as a leader and influencer.

Middleton's dedication to personal growth and development is reflected in his continuous pursuit of new challenges. Whether it's participating in extreme sports, undertaking new expeditions, or exploring innovative business ventures, he consistently pushes the boundaries of what is possible. His willingness to step outside his comfort zone and embrace the unknown serves as a powerful example for others.

Beyond his professional endeavors, Middleton remains committed to various charitable causes. He actively supports organizations that work with veterans, underprivileged youth, and mental health initiatives. His involvement in these causes underscores his belief in giving back and making a positive difference in the lives of others.

As Middleton looks to the future, he envisions expanding his impact through new projects and collaborations. He aims to continue sharing his story and the lessons he has learned, inspiring individuals from all walks of life to overcome their challenges and pursue their dreams with unwavering determination.

Anthony Middleton's life is a testament to the power of resilience, leadership, and the relentless pursuit of excellence. From his early days in the British Army to his rise as a celebrated adventurer and television personality, Middleton has consistently demonstrated the qualities of a true leader. His story is not just one of personal achievement but also one of empowering others to discover their potential and live without limits.

In summary, Anthony Middleton's remarkable journey from soldier to adventurer, author, and motivational speaker highlights his unwavering commitment to excellence and personal growth. His diverse achievements and dedication to helping others continue to inspire and motivate people around the world. Through his adventures, teachings, and charitable work, Middleton's legacy as a resilient and transformative figure endures, encouraging all to face life's challenges with courage and determination.

Anthony Middleton's journey continues to unfold, with each chapter marked by new challenges and achievements. His latest ventures showcase his ever-evolving approach to life and his unyielding dedication to pushing boundaries.

In 2023, Middleton took on a new challenge by starring in the film "Shelter," directed by Scott Vickers. This move into acting allowed him to explore a different aspect of storytelling, bringing his unique perspective and intense experiences to the big screen. The film, which focuses on survival and resilience, resonated deeply with Middleton's own life story, adding yet another layer to his multifaceted career.

Middleton's impact on television remains strong as he continues to host the Australian version of "SAS: Who Dares Wins" and the reality adventure show "Million Dollar Island" for the Seven Network. These roles allow him to mentor and challenge participants, drawing on his vast experience and knowledge to push them to their limits. His presence on these shows not only entertains but also educates viewers about the importance of mental toughness, teamwork, and leadership.

His literary contributions have not slowed down either. Middleton's "Mindset Trilogy," consisting of "First Man In: Leading from the Front," "The Fear Bubble: Harness Fear and Live Without Limits," and "Zero Negativity: The Power of Positive Thinking," continues to inspire readers worldwide. These books delve into the principles that have guided Middleton throughout his life, offering practical advice and motivation for anyone seeking to overcome their fears and achieve their goals.

In addition to his writing, Middleton remains a sought-after speaker, delivering powerful talks on leadership, resilience, and mental fitness. His ability to connect with audiences and share his experiences in a relatable and impactful way has made him a favorite at conferences, corporate events, and motivational seminars.

Middleton's personal life, though often kept private, reflects his core values of loyalty, courage, and perseverance. His family remains a source of strength and support, grounding him as he navigates the demands of his career. Despite the challenges and controversies he has faced, Middleton's commitment to his principles and his dedication to making a positive impact on others have never wavered.

Looking ahead, Middleton has ambitious plans for the future. He envisions expanding the "Ant Middleton Adventure Academy" to reach a global audience, offering transformative experiences that teach resilience, leadership, and survival skills. He also aims to explore new frontiers in television and film, bringing his unique perspective to a broader range of projects.

Moreover, Middleton's philanthropic efforts are set to grow, with plans to establish foundations and initiatives that support veterans, underprivileged youth, and mental health awareness. His belief in giving back and making a positive difference drives these efforts, ensuring that his legacy extends beyond his personal achievements.

Anthony Middleton's story is one of relentless pursuit, resilience, and transformation. From his early days in the British Army to his rise as a celebrated adventurer, author, and television personality, Middleton has consistently demonstrated the qualities of a true leader. His journey inspires countless individuals to face their challenges head-on, embrace their fears, and strive for greatness.

As Middleton continues to break new ground and inspire others, his legacy as a resilient and transformative figure endures. His story serves as a powerful reminder that with determination, courage, and a positive mindset, we can overcome any obstacle and achieve extraordinary things. Anthony Middleton's life is a testament to the power of perseverance and the limitless potential within each of us.

As Anthony Middleton continues to navigate his multifaceted career, his influence and legacy only grow stronger. He remains a symbol of resilience, determination, and the power of a positive mindset. Middleton's journey from a young recruit in the British Army to a celebrated figure in adventure and television is marked by countless milestones and achievements, each contributing to his remarkable story.

In recent years, Middleton has expanded his reach through various digital platforms. His engaging presence on social media allows him to connect with a global audience, sharing insights, motivational content, and glimpses into his adventurous life. Through Instagram, YouTube, and other channels, he inspires millions with his message of pushing boundaries and living life to the fullest.

One of Middleton's most ambitious projects is the development of a comprehensive online training program. This platform offers courses and workshops designed to teach resilience, leadership, and survival skills to people from all walks of life. By leveraging technology, Middleton aims to make his teachings accessible to a wider audience, empowering individuals to overcome their personal challenges and achieve their goals.
Middleton's commitment to adventure and exploration remains unwavering. He continues to undertake daring expeditions, each pushing him to new limits and providing fresh material for his books and television shows. These adventures not only satisfy his personal thirst for challenge but also serve as powerful metaphors for life's struggles, reinforcing his core message of resilience and perseverance.

In addition to his solo ventures, Middleton frequently collaborates with other renowned adventurers and experts. These partnerships result in unique projects that blend diverse perspectives and skills, offering richer and more comprehensive content to his audience. Whether through co-hosted shows, joint expeditions, or collaborative books, these endeavors showcase Middleton's ability to work with others while remaining true to his individual vision.

Middleton's influence extends to the corporate world, where he is a sought-after consultant and speaker. His expertise in leadership and team dynamics is highly valued by businesses looking to foster a culture of resilience and high performance. Through workshops, keynote speeches, and bespoke training programs, Middleton helps organizations build strong, effective teams capable of navigating the complexities of today's business environment.

Despite his numerous professional commitments, Middleton remains dedicated to his family and personal well-being. He prioritizes time with his loved ones, finding balance in the midst of his hectic schedule. His ability to juggle multiple roles while maintaining a strong family foundation is a testament to his disciplined approach and unwavering values.

Middleton's philanthropic efforts continue to expand, with a focus on supporting veterans, mental health initiatives, and underprivileged communities. His work with various charities and organizations highlights his commitment to giving back and making a positive impact on society. Through fundraising events, awareness campaigns, and hands-on involvement, Middleton strives to create meaningful change and support those in need.

Looking to the future, Middleton envisions a legacy that transcends his personal achievements. He aims to inspire future generations of adventurers, leaders, and change-makers, encouraging them to embrace challenges and live their lives with purpose and determination. His story serves as a powerful reminder that with the right mindset, anything is possible.

Anthony Middleton's life is a testament to the extraordinary power of resilience, leadership, and a positive attitude. His journey, marked by countless challenges and triumphs, continues to inspire and motivate people around the world. As he forges ahead with new projects and adventures, Middleton's legacy as a transformative figure remains firmly intact, encouraging all to push beyond their limits and achieve greatness.

Anthony Middleton's influence and impact are ever-expanding, touching lives across various domains. His commitment to pushing boundaries, both personally and professionally, ensures that his legacy will endure for generations to come.

As Middleton continues to share his experiences and insights, he also focuses on mentoring the next generation of adventurers and leaders. He frequently conducts training camps and workshops for young people, particularly those from disadvantaged backgrounds, instilling in them the values of resilience, courage, and perseverance. These programs not only teach practical skills but also build confidence and inspire a sense of possibility in participants.

In the realm of media, Middleton's storytelling prowess remains unmatched. He is currently developing a new documentary series that will take viewers on a journey through some of the world's most extreme environments. This series aims to highlight the beauty and danger of these locations while also emphasizing the importance of environmental conservation. Middleton's ability to combine adventure with a powerful message makes this project highly anticipated by fans and environmentalists alike.

Middleton's entrepreneurial spirit is also evident in his business ventures. He has launched a line of outdoor gear and survival equipment, designed to meet the needs of both amateur enthusiasts and seasoned adventurers. Each product reflects Middleton's extensive experience and is crafted to withstand the rigors of extreme conditions. This venture not only provides high-quality gear but also promotes the ethos of preparedness and resilience that Middleton embodies.

In his personal life, Middleton continues to explore new hobbies and interests, finding balance and fulfillment outside of his demanding career. He is an avid reader, often delving into books on philosophy, history, and leadership, seeking to expand his knowledge and understanding of the world. These pursuits not only enrich his personal life but also inform his professional endeavors, allowing him to bring a well-rounded perspective to his work.
Middleton's dedication to mental health advocacy remains a cornerstone of his public outreach. He actively participates in campaigns and initiatives aimed at breaking the stigma surrounding mental health issues, particularly within the military and veteran communities. His openness about his own struggles and the coping strategies he has developed serves as a beacon of hope and inspiration for others facing similar challenges.

In recognition of his contributions, Middleton has received numerous accolades and awards. These honors celebrate his achievements in the fields of adventure, television, and philanthropy, cementing his status as a respected and influential figure. Yet, despite these accolades, Middleton remains grounded and focused on his mission to inspire and empower others.
Looking ahead, Middleton is set to release a new book that delves deeper into the philosophy of resilience. This book will explore the mental and emotional aspects of overcoming adversity, offering readers practical tools and insights to apply in their own lives. As with his previous works, this book is expected to resonate deeply with readers, providing them with the guidance and motivation needed to navigate their personal journeys.

As Anthony Middleton continues to forge new paths and take on new challenges, his story serves as a powerful testament to the strength of the human spirit. His unwavering dedication to excellence, combined with his genuine desire to help others, ensures that his legacy will be one of lasting impact and inspiration. Through his adventures, writings, and public outreach, Middleton continues to demonstrate that with courage, resilience, and a positive mindset, we can all achieve extraordinary things.

Anthony Middleton's journey is a saga of relentless pursuit of excellence, constant reinvention, and profound impact. As he looks to the future, several exciting projects and initiatives are on the horizon, each promising to further extend his influence and reach.

One of Middleton's most ambitious endeavors is the establishment of a global resilience training academy. This institution aims to provide comprehensive training programs that cover physical endurance, mental toughness, and leadership skills. The academy will offer both in-person and online courses, making it accessible to a diverse, international audience. Through this initiative, Middleton hopes to create a community of resilient individuals equipped to handle the challenges of modern life with grace and strength.

Middleton's passion for storytelling is also set to take a new turn with the development of a feature film based on his life. This project, still in its early stages, aims to capture the essence of his extraordinary journey from a troubled youth to a celebrated adventurer and public figure. The film will explore the pivotal moments that shaped him, the challenges he faced, and the triumphs he achieved, providing an intimate and inspiring portrait of his life.

In addition to his ventures in training and media, Middleton is committed to continuing his philanthropic work. He is in the process of setting up a charitable foundation that will support veterans, mental health initiatives, and disadvantaged youth. The foundation will fund programs that provide education, therapy, and support services, aiming to empower individuals and communities to overcome their challenges and thrive.

Middleton's personal life remains a source of joy and fulfillment. He is deeply involved in his children's lives, instilling in them the same values of resilience and determination that have guided him. Family adventures and explorations continue to be a significant part of their lives, fostering a strong bond and shared love for the outdoors.

His relationship with his wife remains a cornerstone of his stability and happiness. Together, they navigate the complexities of public life, supporting each other's endeavors and maintaining a strong, loving partnership. Middleton often credits his family's unwavering support as a crucial element of his success, highlighting the importance of a solid foundation in achieving one's dreams.

Middleton's influence is also growing in the corporate world. His leadership seminars and keynote speeches are in high demand, with organizations across the globe seeking his insights on building resilient teams and fostering a culture of excellence. His ability to translate his military and adventure experiences into practical lessons for the business world has made him a sought-after consultant and speaker.

As he continues to expand his reach, Middleton remains committed to personal growth and self-improvement. He regularly seeks out new challenges, both physical and mental, to push his limits and evolve as an individual. Whether it's training for an ultra-marathon, studying a new discipline, or embarking on a solo expedition, Middleton's quest for growth is unending.

His upcoming autobiography, tentatively titled "Beyond the Fear Bubble," promises to delve deeper into his philosophy of life. This book will explore the concept of fear and how to harness it as a powerful force for personal transformation. Drawing on his own experiences and the stories of others who have overcome significant challenges, Middleton aims to provide readers with a roadmap to living fearlessly and fulfilling their potential.

In every aspect of his life, Anthony Middleton exemplifies the qualities of a true adventurer and leader. His story is a testament to the power of resilience, the importance of a positive mindset, and the impact one individual can have on the world. As he continues to inspire and empower people globally, Middleton's legacy as a transformative figure in adventure, leadership, and personal development is assured.

With each new challenge he undertakes and every life he touches, Middleton reaffirms his commitment to living boldly and authentically. His journey is far from over, and as he continues to explore new horizons and inspire others, the world eagerly awaits the next chapter in the extraordinary life of Anthony Middleton.

Anthony Middleton's future is as adventurous and inspiring as his past. As he ventures into new territories, his journey continues to be a beacon of hope and motivation for countless individuals.

Middleton's global resilience training academy, which is set to launch soon, is poised to become a hub for aspiring adventurers and leaders. The academy will offer a diverse range of programs, from intensive boot camps to long-term leadership courses, all designed to push participants to their limits and help them discover their true potential. With state-of-the-art facilities and a team of experienced instructors, Middleton aims to create an environment that nurtures growth, fosters camaraderie, and instills a sense of discipline and purpose.

The feature film based on Middleton's life is gaining momentum, with a talented team of writers and producers dedicated to bringing his story to the big screen. This film will not only entertain but also educate audiences about the values of perseverance, courage, and resilience. It will delve into the challenges Middleton faced, including his time in the military, his personal struggles, and his rise to fame. By sharing his story, Middleton hopes to inspire viewers to overcome their own obstacles and pursue their dreams with unwavering determination.

Middleton's charitable foundation is already making a significant impact. The foundation's initiatives focus on providing resources and support to veterans transitioning to civilian life, offering mental health services, and creating educational opportunities for disadvantaged youth. Middleton personally oversees many of the foundation's projects, ensuring that they align with his vision of empowerment and positive change. His dedication to giving back to the community is a testament to his character and his commitment to making a difference.

In his personal life, Middleton continues to cherish the time he spends with his family. Family adventures remain a staple, whether it's exploring remote wilderness areas or engaging in thrilling outdoor activities. These experiences not only strengthen their bond but also instill a love for nature and adventure in his children. Middleton and his wife have also become advocates for family wellness, often sharing tips and insights on maintaining a healthy, active lifestyle.

Middleton's role as a motivational speaker and corporate consultant is flourishing. Companies from various industries seek his expertise in building resilient teams and fostering a culture of excellence. His dynamic presentations, filled with real-life anecdotes and actionable strategies, leave a lasting impact on audiences. Middleton's ability to connect with people on a personal level and convey complex concepts in an engaging manner makes him a standout figure in the world of motivational speaking.

As part of his continuous personal growth, Middleton has taken up new hobbies that challenge both his body and mind. He has developed a keen interest in martial arts, finding that the discipline and focus required complement his overall philosophy of life. Additionally, he has begun studying mindfulness and meditation, integrating these practices into his daily routine to maintain balance and mental clarity amidst his busy schedule.

Middleton's upcoming autobiography, "Beyond the Fear Bubble," is eagerly anticipated by his fans. This book promises to be a deep dive into his philosophy of harnessing fear to fuel personal transformation. It will feature insights from his own life, as well as stories from individuals he has encountered who have overcome significant challenges. By sharing these narratives, Middleton aims to provide readers with practical tools and inspiration to face their fears and achieve their goals.

In every endeavor, Anthony Middleton exemplifies the spirit of a true adventurer and leader. His unwavering commitment to pushing boundaries, his dedication to helping others, and his relentless pursuit of personal growth ensure that his legacy will continue to inspire for years to come. As he embarks on new challenges and explores uncharted territories, the world watches with admiration and anticipation, knowing that Middleton's journey is far from over and that his impact will be felt for generations.

Anthony Middleton's impact extends beyond the tangible achievements of his career. His story is one of transformation, resilience, and the unyielding human spirit. As he looks to the future, he remains committed to pushing his limits and exploring new avenues to inspire and motivate others.

Middleton's work in the realm of mental health advocacy is gaining significant traction. Understanding the critical importance of mental well-being, especially for veterans and individuals in high-stress environments, he is developing a comprehensive mental health program. This initiative aims to provide accessible resources, support networks, and counseling services to those in need. By leveraging his platform and personal experiences, Middleton hopes to break down the stigma surrounding mental health issues and encourage people to seek help and support.

His global resilience training academy is not just about physical endurance; it encompasses holistic development, including mental strength and emotional intelligence. The curriculum includes workshops on mindfulness, stress management, and adaptive leadership, equipping participants with the skills needed to thrive in any situation. Middleton's hands-on approach and personal involvement in the training sessions ensure that each participant receives guidance and mentorship, fostering a supportive and empowering community.

The feature film on Middleton's life is evolving into a multi-faceted project. In addition to the movie, there are plans for a documentary series that delves deeper into specific aspects of his journey, including his military service, his time in the Special Boat Service, and his experiences in television. This series will provide a more nuanced and detailed exploration of his life, offering viewers a comprehensive understanding of the man behind the public persona.

Middleton's charitable foundation is expanding its reach, partnering with organizations worldwide to amplify its impact. Initiatives are being launched in various regions, focusing on education, mental health, and community development. One notable project is the establishment of educational centers in underserved areas, providing children with access to quality education and extracurricular activities. These centers aim to nurture talent, encourage creativity, and foster a love for learning, giving children the tools they need to build a brighter future.

Middleton's personal life continues to be a source of strength and inspiration. He and his wife have become advocates for family wellness, often sharing their journey of maintaining a balanced and healthy family life amidst their busy careers. They host workshops and webinars on family dynamics, stress management, and the importance of spending quality time together. Their commitment to family values resonates with many, offering practical advice and heartfelt insights.

As a motivational speaker, Middleton's influence is expanding globally. He is frequently invited to speak at international conferences, corporate events, and educational institutions. His talks, characterized by authenticity and relatability, leave a lasting impression on audiences. He shares not only his successes but also his failures, emphasizing the lessons learned and the importance of resilience and perseverance.

Middleton's personal growth journey is ongoing. He continues to challenge himself physically and mentally, taking on new adventures and learning new skills. His exploration into martial arts has deepened, with Middleton achieving significant milestones and even participating in competitions. His dedication to mindfulness and meditation has also grown, leading him to explore different practices and philosophies from around the world.

The release of "Beyond the Fear Bubble" is highly anticipated. This book is expected to be a transformative guide for readers, offering practical strategies for facing and overcoming fear. Middleton's honest and candid writing style, combined with his wealth of experiences, promises to provide readers with invaluable insights and motivation. The book will be accompanied by a series of workshops and seminars, allowing readers to engage with Middleton directly and apply the principles outlined in the book to their own lives.

In every aspect of his life, Anthony Middleton continues to embody the qualities of a true adventurer and leader. His relentless pursuit of excellence, his dedication to helping others, and his unwavering commitment to personal growth ensure that his influence will be felt for generations to come. As he embarks on new challenges and explores uncharted territories, the world watches with admiration and anticipation, knowing that Middleton's journey is far from over and that his impact will only continue to grow.

As Anthony Middleton moves forward, his influence is expanding into new, innovative domains. His dedication to personal development and helping others achieve their potential remains at the forefront of his endeavors. Here are some of the exciting ventures and initiatives that lie ahead in Middleton's extraordinary journey:

Expanding the Global Resilience Training Academy

The Global Resilience Training Academy, Middleton's brainchild, is on the brink of launching satellite campuses in key locations around the world. These campuses will be strategically placed in areas known for their challenging environments, such as the Rocky Mountains in the USA, the Outback in Australia, and the Andes in South America. Each location will offer specialized programs tailored to the unique geographical and cultural aspects of the region. This expansion aims to make resilience training accessible to a broader audience, fostering a global network of empowered individuals.

Television and Digital Media

Middleton's foray into television continues to grow, with several new projects in development. He is set to produce and host a new documentary series that explores the untold stories of unsung heroes from various walks of life. This series will highlight the resilience and courage of individuals who have overcome significant adversity, providing viewers with both inspiration and practical life lessons.

In addition, Middleton is developing a podcast that will delve into themes of leadership, mental toughness, and personal growth. The podcast will feature in-depth interviews with thought leaders, athletes, and military veterans, offering listeners a wealth of knowledge and actionable advice. By leveraging the power of digital media, Middleton aims to reach a wider audience and create a platform for meaningful conversations.

Innovative Mental Health Initiatives

Understanding the importance of mental health, especially for those in high-stress professions, Middleton is launching a groundbreaking mental health initiative. This program will utilize virtual reality (VR) technology to create immersive therapeutic experiences. Participants will be able to engage in VR scenarios designed to reduce stress, improve mental resilience, and provide coping strategies for anxiety and trauma. This cutting-edge approach aims to revolutionize the way mental health support is delivered, making it more engaging and effective.

Adventure Expeditions and Public Engagements

Middleton continues to push the boundaries of adventure, planning a series of high-profile expeditions that will be documented for television and digital platforms. These expeditions include a daring journey to the North Pole, an exploration of the Amazon Rainforest, and a challenging trek across the Sahara Desert. Each adventure will not only test Middleton's limits but also serve as a platform to raise awareness for environmental conservation and support for veteran charities.

Public engagements remain a crucial part of Middleton's mission. He regularly participates in speaking tours, both in-person and virtually, where he shares his experiences and insights with audiences worldwide. His dynamic and motivational presentations continue to inspire and empower individuals to embrace challenges and pursue their dreams.

Community and Philanthropy

Middleton's charitable foundation is broadening its scope, with new initiatives aimed at supporting underprivileged communities. One significant project involves partnering with local organizations to build community centers in impoverished areas. These centers will offer educational programs, vocational training, and recreational activities, providing residents with valuable resources and opportunities for growth.

In addition to his foundation's work, Middleton actively supports several global causes. He is an ambassador for environmental conservation, advocating for sustainable practices and the protection of endangered species. His involvement in these causes underscores his commitment to making a positive impact on the world.

Personal Growth and Family Life

Middleton's personal journey continues to be one of growth and self-discovery. He remains dedicated to his martial arts practice, achieving new belts and competing at higher levels. His exploration of mindfulness and meditation has led him to study under renowned teachers, deepening his understanding of these practices and incorporating them into his daily life.

Family remains at the heart of Middleton's life. He and his wife have authored a book on family wellness, sharing their experiences and strategies for maintaining a balanced and fulfilling family life. They continue to embark on family adventures, fostering a love for nature and adventure in their children. Their shared commitment to family values and well-being serves as an inspiration to many.

Writing and Publications

Middleton's writing career is flourishing. His upcoming book, "Beyond the Fear Bubble," is already generating excitement. In addition to this book, he has plans for a series of children's books that teach resilience, teamwork, and the importance of a positive mindset. These books aim to inspire young readers and provide them with the tools to navigate life's challenges.

His previously published books continue to resonate with readers worldwide, offering insights into leadership, personal growth, and overcoming fear. Middleton frequently hosts book signings and interactive workshops, where he engages with readers and shares deeper insights into the themes explored in his books.

A Legacy of Inspiration

Anthony Middleton's journey is far from over. His relentless pursuit of excellence, his dedication to helping others, and his unwavering commitment to personal growth ensure that his influence will continue to expand. Middleton's story is one of transformation and resilience, a testament to the power of the human spirit. As he embarks on new challenges and explores uncharted territories, the world watches with admiration and anticipation, knowing that Middleton's legacy will continue to inspire for generations to come.

Printed in Great Britain
by Amazon

53498685R00020